VIOLENCE: METAMORPHOSIS

Violence: Metamorphosis

A collection of poems
by
KYLE DOTY

Adelaide Books
New York / Lisbon
2020

VIOLENCE: METAMORPHOSIS
A collection of poems
By Kyle Doty

Copyright © by Kyle Doty
Cover design © 2020 Adelaide Books

Published by Adelaide Books, New York / Lisbon
adelaidebooks.org

Editor-in-Chief
Stevan V. Nikolic

All rights reserved. No part of this book may be reproduced in any manner whatsoever without written permission from the author except in the case of brief quotations embodied in critical articles and reviews.

For any information, please address Adelaide Books
at info@adelaidebooks.org
or write to:
Adelaide Books
244 Fifth Ave. Suite D27
New York, NY, 10001

ISBN: 978-1-953510-30-3

Printed in the United States of America

For Sharayah.

Also, for Darin and Lona.

Contents

Acknowledgements   *11*

Terse Cerebrations   *13*

We Suffer Violence   *14*

Ceiling Fan   *15*

Another Poem About Tragedy   *16*

One True Holy Faith   *17*

Natus   *18*

I Fear the River   *19*

Grip   *20*

The Lamp Post   *21*

October 4, 2018   *22*

Different Acts Same Scene   *23*

Between Midnight and Three   *25*

Mourner's Curse *26*

Coming Home from the Doctor *27*

Fort Myers, Circa 2005 *28*

Dust to Dust *29*

The Sound of Violin in the Dark *30*

Showers *31*

Sariye *32*

The Garden *33*

Natus *34*

Martelé *35*

When the Children Died *37*

October *39*

Summertime *41*

For Ginsberg *42*

Making Coffee, Midsummer Morning *44*

Han *45*

Instructions *46*

Five Month Triptych *47*

Thirty-four *50*

VIOLENCE: METAMORPHOSIS

Irma *51*

Gemellos *52*

The Squirrels in the Yard *53*

Arcadia *54*

Splash Pad *55*

The Cat the Nightmaid *56*

Silhouette *57*

Insomnia *58*

The Picture *59*

The Cat Doesn't Like Being Shut Out. *60*

Morning Precipitation *61*

12.31.17 *62*

Violence: Metamorphosis *63*

About the Author *65*

Acknowledgements

Thank you to Sharayah and the kids for giving me the time to sit in the office and write this. Also, thank you to Katie Horst, Sarah Richardson, Melodie Robelo, Tim Goodman, and Terri Golden for being first readers. Thank you, again, Sarah Richardson for tackling the editing process with me. Finally, thanks to Louise Glück for writing "A Village Life" and "Ararat," which are constant companions and sources of inspiration.

The poems "Ceiling Fan," "Five Month Tryptich," and "Another Poem About Tragedy" first appeared in Adelaide Literary Magazine.

Terse Cerebrations

because you taught me what love was
I spent that winter staring into the vapid
eyes of a man-kid turned monster.

in some supernal way our
strange pair's a twisted root rot.

one flesh.

each one the other's phantom limb.

We Suffer Violence

It was summer and the summer was violent.

And then it was fall.
    Fall was less violent.
It was like Sun Ra: you go through metamorphosis.
    You adjust to the

change that was forced upon you.

You adjust to the savagery and let it work its way
through you like yeast through dough.

It wasn't the orb of the sun bolted in the clear sky—
an eye, unblinking, unwavering in its intensity
that changed us.

It was nothing like that.
It was like this:

It was the cool moon.
Its webby light that drenched us.

We weren't looking and it did us in.

A thief in the night peeking through the open window.
It did us in when we were least expecting it.

With the wind came a spirit and with the spirit
came the terror: change that forces change.

Ceiling Fan

Your long vulnerable body, asleep,
presents itself like someone
timid for affection—
me feeling like a voyeur,
a purveyor of skin.

I've witnessed the terror of
you sleeping alone, your back
to your lover—your exotic
dreams the only sensuous touch.

And when you're not alone,
in a tangle of arms and feet,
your mouth hole open exposing
the blackness of your throat,
from which escapes the short

sounds of ecstasy—I, a prophet,
can see you're still alone—

trapped in some locked-away
suffering.

Another Poem About Tragedy

I told you your sins were absolved.
I did not tell you that I don't have the authority.
So I'm a liar.

The truth is without you there wouldn't be a tragedy. If my life were a film, you'd be the antagonist with a sinister smile, always a trick up your sleeve; it's because in the film you'd have already emptied the contents of the vault into your bag and for the duration of the story they'd be picking through clues to find you.

But once they find you, film's over. It's because there's nothing left to see. Who wants to watch a film with no bad guy? No one goes to see a movie where nothing happens.

Like I said, you bring the tragedy.

All I do is play priest after the bad deed is done and deliver you the news that it was all a fraud.

One True Holy Faith

As teenagers dream of getting laid for the first time after the
big homecoming dance, fall slides into the blank space on
the calendar mocking summer with its heat and promise of
picnics and sweaty love affairs.

Here it's still just as hot as it was in July, and our eyes are
once again transfixed on the Atlantic at the swirling masses
of cancer threatening to metastasize and infect us like
last summer.

The plants in the garden hunker down.
Their roots double down deep in search of safety.
There's so much violence here.
We cling to faith that God will spare us.

The plants, too, trust the Earth will hold them in its grip and
supply a fair share of water.

Natus

With the first soft flurries came the long fingers of pain.

By the time the world was white, it was time to
go. The roads were cordoned off in places. So early
in the morning, most people were home, still in bed,
under thick comforters, electric blankets; men asleep,
nude, pressing themselves against their lovers.

The deserted streets under the cold glow of the moon must
have been something to see: radiant glory, trees illuminated
by light and ice the way a cobweb reflects morning sun.

I came screaming into the sterile light.

I had not mastered anything. I had not tasted the acidity
of hate. I did not, because I could not, feel the fire of love.

I was the only one. There was no one in my universe, yet.

For a while, under a heat lamp, a small cotton
hat atop my head the shape of a cone because
I was plunged from darkness, I was still.

Then I was taken to my mother.

I Fear the River

Like a demoniac,
breathless scurrying across detritus,
the river rises.

Anxiety asphyxiates.

At night I lay in bed
and listen past the whir of the
ceiling fan to the river—

it rises and falls like a man's
chest during sleep. The
breath shallow then deep.

Sometimes rhythm is torture.

One night the river will wake
and crawl up and over its banks.
Wicked, sharp-toothed, strangled
breath up dead throat—
the river will rise

and pile itself at the front door
knocking like deception and
creep through the cracks and

windows until I'm inundated.

Grip

Most days I rise early before light twists
free and tears across Arcadia.
When I rise, I do not take my walk, not
while it's dark. The best I do is
stand on the porch with my coffee and
watch the men leave for work.

Today before nine I had part of the garden
ripped up, its remnants dumped
behind the garage, and plans to plant
flowers or pennisetum around the
lamp post.

Pulling up the old bushes around the
lamp post, I considered the
Earth and its grip on what it takes inside
itself. The Earth does not have want.
What it takes in, it owns.

The root of a bush, for example.
For another, the carrion of a beloved.

The Lamp Post

A garden does not prefer to know the name of anyone
who, at night under a milky moon,
wanders its flagstone path.

It's like the cat who's stretched out in the window taking in
sun. It knows it'll be tended to. The garden expects this.

The man and woman who tend the garden, together, do so in
solitude. One digging up Milkweed, the
other cutting grass, transplanting

shrubs, flowers. I have seen others, the
same, side by side, their parallel work
signifying that each one is trying to make
the other happy. Because he

didn't bring home Bromeliads, he's
thinking of her. They don't see
themselves, arms loaded with rough torn
weeds. If you don't get the root,

they'll return and choke the new flowers.

October 4, 2018

Light jolts the hallowed ground
after breaking from the sun and
punching its way through the
broad swath of trees.

The trees don't feel the violence of it.

They don't see the light as exposure.

The light spills through the window
in my office, soaking my bare feet.

I switch off the lamp and it makes
no difference.

Different Acts Same Scene

The man wakes early when the night still holds the world in an iron grip.
He's worked this way for as long as he can remember. Rise at dark and return at dark.
He doesn't recognize the property when it's flooded by the raw light of the sun.
Sometimes there's a woman in the bed. She shifts and stretches when he untangles himself from her petite frame.
The women—they come and go.
They are all the same.
Small, anxious birds—they all need him.
They need his strength, his clarity of mind.
But they don't last.

At first, things are fine. The women tell their friends about him—his charm, his dimples, the way his throat looks when he's freshly shaven and wearing a bright button down shirt.
They sip wine and fuss over how he clears his throat before he says I love you like it makes him uncomfortable to be romantic.
    It's cute he's willing.

Soon the women realize he's reciting from some script he's perfected.
They know after the third or fourth I love you that he's methodical.
He could be reading lines.
Ticking off a box on a to-do list.

Sometimes he ends things first. But only when the woman doesn't get it.
Doesn't get that he's not serious.
Other times he returns home after dusk to find the house empty save for the cat crying for dinner. None of the women leave on their own volition without feeding the cat. It's just always late—the cat's been waiting awhile.
When they leave because he's said so, it's different. He helps them pack their two drawers and bathroom belongings. He'll drive them away if they don't have a car or he'll stand in the driveway and wave goodbye as though she's only departing for awhile.
They always leave loving him and knowing he never actually existed. His body was there but him—he wasn't real.
And always he sits alone with a drink and scratches the cat between the ears, sips and stares out the window until it's time for bed.
He doesn't smell the woman's pillow or long for her warm body to cling to him. He just sleeps and wakes and moves onto the next act.

Between Midnight and Three

It was raining.
The sound of it made me think
of small stars that plink from sky onto metal roof.

In the dark I lie, half covered by the blue down comforter,
staring at the ceiling imagining each star bouncing off
the roof and landing in the sea.

Down on the beach lovers cuddled.
Warmed by blanket and fire, they discuss
the species of fish that could make such a splash.

I'd been dreaming. The dream was always the same.
I was alone and old, cleaning up after dinner.

Standing at the kitchen sink, looking out the window
overlooking the garden, I was washing my plate,
my wine glass, a fork and spoon.

To the flower vender at the farmer's market I said:
I don't know why I have so many dishes. I use the
same ones each meal, wash them, and put them away.

Mourner's Curse

The impatiens have died in their pots. Every one
of them fallen over limp like dead cartoon soldiers.

In one pot two lizards run through the flopsy stems
chasing in a mating game as if the dead mean nothing.

Irreverence!

There's just one left standing, but it's wavering.
You can see it in the coloring.

Not unlike us, in the presence of the sick it cannot cease
trying to flourish.

Coming Home from the Doctor

Driving in silence—the fields a blur, abandoned.
Sky awash with grey clouds. From
out of nowhere, rain like an accident
dropped on the windshield.
Just a splash and it was done.

Perhaps Zeus lost his balance, startling
Aetos Dios, causing him to knock over a pitcher of
icewater.

Fort Myers, Circa 2005

That winter before the time change when it still got dark
early and the weather was still cool, the guys, one evening
while we were serving fried fish baskets to tourists at Shrimp
Shack, put all the living room furniture
on the roof and arranged
it as it had been in the room below.

Our headlights swept across the driveway and revealed the
joke and our wonder at the magnificence of it.
Before that, you girls filled my bathtub with noodles.

That winter I got high on Sam's painkillers for the first time
to mute the lonely flower taking root.

While everyone laughed and marveled at how those guys
got the furniture—sofa and all—up on the roof, I stared up
at the clear raven sky, dotted with pin pricks of white
brilliant light and wondered what planet I must be from—

The laughter escaping my mouth sounded light years
away.

Dust to Dust

I wasn't taught to fear death.
In our house, death was always on
the other end of the phone.
All it took to make my mother cry was for her to hear
the hitch in someone's voice, words trapped
in the throat and belched up like fire.
For my mother to worry, all it took was for the phone to ring.

As though ignoring the dead silenced
the act of death, my father
seemed not to notice.
A working hypothesis: if you give attention
to death, it won't touch you.

In summer the cemetery is shaded in green light.
It's blue and cold during winter.
You lay spouses next to one another. If this is
the one who died first, the living one looks at their
name carved into the granite—a
beginning date, not yet an end.
You must think: this I cannot escape.

Someone drops a handful of dirt into the open grave.
The women cry. The men, like dad, just stand, backs
rigid and try not to notice the pile of dirt, tarp covered,
out in the distance. When everyone
turns to leave, the wind picks
up and dirt blows in our eyes.

The Sound of Violin in the Dark

There you are—
       standing at the counter in the
dark kitchen, having returned from
the haunted mansion wearing a
mask.

You're showing us how you'd
greet your guests had you had
a party this year.

All I notice are your hands—
delicate things, pale, your long
fingers made to stretch the
length of strings while you slide
the bow against them—

Your whole life is making music
where there's only chaos.

One hand rests on another and
I'm thinking how you'll never
hurt me—the promise you
whispered to me in the dark.

You make music, and
my ear is attuned to what you're
trying to drown out.

Showers

It's been raining for weeks.
Not unrelenting rain.
That would be unheard of here.
The rain comes and goes like the widow
who wanders town after
the death of the spouse.
The garden is waterlogged.
The plants are shocked.
Nothing for so long and suddenly a torrent.
The soil isn't used to it. The rain doesn't soak in right away.
It's the way a person reacts to love after so long without.

Sariye

When you're young, you imagine having a family.
When you get one, you learn that
you cannot possess a child just like
you cannot possess the cat who stalks the house at night.

My daughter and I are experts at silence.
She greets the cat and carries him to bed,
and I hope she doesn't think he's her only lifeline.

The Garden

My hands in the sandy soil planting
the Cordyline and Celosia.
The Celosia will die quickly. I don't have luck with those.
I plant them because I have hope. It's
how I show that I still have faith.

The soil is not black and rich.
This is Florida.
Gardening is an act of faith.

Before, when the garden wasn't ours, it was
only green. Now, flowers light
the yard.
But it's still green, predominantly.

I hate to see flowers die.

Natus

To be a child means to not be in control of your life.
When you're inside your mother, the only sound
is the beating of her heart.
To get born is not your decision.
Something other than mother chooses.
At once you see light when all you've endured is shadows,
and you're placed in the arms of strangers and passed to a
stranger.

I had a dream I was alone, a baby, lying on a rock—a small
blue blanket draped across my middle the way it's done in
paintings of saintly children.

There were no soft lullabies.

There were wild animals near.
I could hear the howling and
ragged breath of beasts with claws.
Someone came to me, and picked me up.
I nursed from a beast with wings.
There were roses in her coarse hair.

Upon waking, in a crib, in a light filled room, I heard my
own cries as the cries of another. Someone came and lifted
me, and I recognized her as mother.

For Jada

Martelé

A downpour at dusk. The sound of cars
passing by like a mother shushing her
young in a dark nursery.

Late summer: the evenings getting cool
enough for a sweater.
Stars settling into place
even before the last breath
of sun sinks away to someplace not here.

The sound of your violin screams through
the air, carried on the wing of a vulture.
Something violent is born.

To watch you play in the middle of the room—your eyes
turned to coal, your lips forming a
perfect O—is to watch a tragedy.

I'm told to boil a frog alive you put
it in cool water and slowly
turn up the heat. That's your tragedy: you can't tell the
heat's been turned up.

You make the violin scream to match
the sound you make when you
wake from the only nightmare you
have. The one where you become

Kyle Doty

a monster: your light eyes turn dark:
your vision becomes dark;
the music is frantic like the rhythm of your heart.

You're driven by the drum of your pulse
behind your soft temples.

I tell myself I can escape.
I harm myself with hope.

My heart is a tiny pebble of iron;
your violin is a magnet.

When the Children Died

When the children died,
and you along with them,
I chose to stay alone.

I woke each day with the
sun forcing its way through
the slats of the blinds

and made coffee before feeding
the cat and reading the Times
on the porch.

I worked in silence save for
the cat who wandered room
to room searching, ears back

and alert, waiting for the girl
child to leap out at him.
Evenings before dark, when

the sky like canvas was painted
by a blaze of low light, I'd
switch on the lights in the house

and not forget the lamp post
in the garden— you told me
it's safer that way. Sauteing vegetables,

Kyle Doty

pictures of the children lined up
on the mantle, I whispered into
the silence that we'll have cookies after dinner.

October

is the last we spoke.
        You offered me your instrument—
your pride and joy.

What I wanted —my life back—
        You couldn't give me.
And so you offered me what you could.

Even then I couldn't take it.
        To cart off with the keyboard
Would have hurt you too much.

I could see it in your eyes.
        You would be lost without the
Ability to make music,

Which was your only way to translate
        What the dark ghost who followed
You was saying.

I thought if you could make music
        You wouldn't need to do what he
Demanded; you'd just turn it into something

Haunting and sad.
        From the front seat of the car,
I could see you standing in the

window playing your
Violin. The sun glinted against the glass,

And you closed your brilliant
Eyes so as not to allow Ra

To defeat the Ares within.

Summertime

You can't keep the flowers alive.
It's because of the heat.

After late morning, you don't go out again
until evening when the sun is low.
Because it's summer, the sun hangs low for hours
before giving up and sinking out of sight.

During the heat of the afternoon, those who are responsible
for children take naps with them. The cat naps taking
a break from playing with his stuffed mouse and
clawing at the chair.

Others do their work or sit quietly in the window and listen
to the flowers fight for life.

For Ginsberg

The sun hangs onto the sky,
white knuckled,
like some climber who's found
himself in a bad place
on the side of some mountain.
And this, for obvious reasons,
reminds me of you.
You are somewhere, not here,
and you're staring at the same sun,
maybe thinking the same thing,
and I wonder if there's a chance you're thinking of me.
You are probably insane now;
although, you either don't know it
or you hide it from those who you've let in—
who have let you in.
You would have to be to be you;
to be the man you became,
you would have to be bat shit crazy
to go on working and living
and finding reasons to go on working and living.
It's not that I wish you unluck
or merciless sleep;
on the contrary, I hope you know you're sanctified.

How sad you were
knowing it was all crashing down
like bricks on your head.

VIOLENCE: METAMORPHOSIS

I've never seen a man drown
except for that day
sometime in October
when I stood aside
and watched you go under
and be pulled by the current of depravity—
angelheaded hipsters burning for the ancient
heavenly connection to the starry dynamo
in the machinery of night had a better shot
at saving themselves than you that day.

When you left for good did you pack a bag?
Did tears fill the corners of your light eyes?
And did you weep because they thought you a monster
or because, for in a lucid moment of sanity, did you
see yourself as one?

*Text in italics is borrowed from
Allen Ginsberg's "Howl (4-5)"

Making Coffee, Midsummer Morning

Did you hear about my brother? he asks in his message.
I'm making coffee, just out of bed and barely dressed.
It's midsummer, so it's not cold; despite the humidity,
my skin dimples in gooseflesh, and I think about the way
it must feel for someone's ghost to pass through them.
You know what it's like for the air to turn cold, your
breath to freeze, and for a moment you're not here but
there—in the pluck of a memory so strong it's involuntary
that you, for just a moment, relive
whatever blackness was then.

No need for me to reply, he's dead set on telling
me anyway; it's gossip, the good kind, family tragedy.
His brother's gone to jail.

Standing over the sink, staring out the small window into
the backyard, I think about the trails you led us down in
search of adventure.
Your long periods of silence I mistook for anger:
I'd not kept up or said the wrong thing.
Were you contemplating your life? Willing me to
stand up and scream at you—that no you cannot possess
me the way the gardner possesses the orchid. Maybe vacillating
between nourishing me or trampling me down with
the sole of your foot.

Han

A flower dies in its pot, the Celosia are uprooted by
an animal, seeds don't sprout.
October doesn't bring a reprieve from the heat.
The child gets sick; the doctor is weary.

Somewhere there's a man sitting alone
on a park bench looking out over the harbor
and wondering if the risk to love another
is worth it after love has failed once.

A child leaves home.
The mother and father stand at the door
and wave until the car has disappeared.
Both notice now their hands—old and vulnerable.

A retirement party
A sheet cake and a single candle
representing twenty years.
There's discussion over who gets his office
with the small window that overlooks the
parking lot.

Han—
A sadness so deep there are no tears;
yet, there is still hope. A dull ache of
the soul.

Instructions

Children aren't born with a set of instructions.
You should know that you do harm if you
show attention to the young child. It means the
older one will feel abandoned again.
The girl child will only take affection for so long.
The quick son will be good at karate and advanced
logical reasoning but fear, at night, the open closet
door and hate to read.
They should caution that you'll wake in the night
and wander the silent house wondering if you
cause irreparable damage by insisting
the middle child eat all her vegetables.

Five Month Triptych

I.   Not yet Independence Day

    The day before July fourth.
    The sun envelops the body in
    its tight fist—
    twenty minutes at the playground
    today was all even the children could bear.

    All the stores are packed with
    holiday shoppers and those who
    just let out of church—it was easy
    to spot the church-goers:
    the children are bundles of energy,
    the mothers' dresses are clean and pressed,
    fathers happy, like the children,
    to be up and moving, ready to eat.

    We visited our friend's baby.
    She slept the whole time.
    First in her mother's lap
    and then in her father's arms.

II. Moved in

    The moving truck was parked
    and reparked three times
    in the driveway—

    a space larger than our front yard
    at the old house. The house that
    maybe still expects us to return

    one day and press our ears to
    her side to hear her secrets—
    Her anxiety because the man

    who enters her each evening
    is still a stranger even though
    it's been three months.

    By near October there are
    still boxes in the corners
    of rooms and the kitchen

    we began remodeling
    is still in shambles.

    The old house sighs so
    deeply I can hear her from
    here.

    It's the sound of children's
    feet slapping against her
    floorboards she misses most.

VIOLENCE: METAMORPHOSIS

III. Academic Year

>Someone once told
>me work is hard by design.
>Adam made it so
>in the garden with
>that apple and his
>lady friend.
>
>Others tell me Christ
>the Eternal Immanuel
>redeemed it all down
>to the single last tittle
>of humanity.

Thirty-four

Born; birth is a transition from
life in black and shadow to
excruciating light— sound like a
thousand bawling waterfalls.

In a moment you go from veiled
idea to tangible, applicable life
filled with the raw light of creation.

You were born and there was laughter
and the awesome sense that something
supernatural had happened.

The sun lay its bovine head for
the evening, and that was your first day.

                        For Sharayah:
                              for your birthday

Irma

The slow pulse of her terrible
heart inched her closer.

Unblinking cyclops
steered by hate
snapped north, a

wobbly trajectory brought
her with her languid spin
over our land.

X marks the spot.

She howled and beat
against the house, tested
the wooden shutters that
took us days to get up.

Lights out.
Unlike me, she didn't think
fences make good neighbors.

The cat curled around our
feet purring, hungry,
as though the sky was
not falling.

Gemellos

They dream about losing each other.

Awake in the night, wide-eyed and searching,
groping in the dark, fistfulls of comforter for
their other—brother who knows, who understands—
same flesh from shared womb.

One day they will not share a bed, too
grown for a single full-size comforter.
One day cars will transport them miles
apart into the arms of another other,

their mother's womb a reliquary of
subconscious memory.

For Ames and Eero

The Squirrels in the Yard

The squirrels in the yard don't wonder if today's
the day they cease to live.
Death doesn't cross their minds like a wrinkle
across their foreheads.
They skitter from place to place showing off
their perfect memory digging up the acorns
they planted weeks ago.

A squirrel doesn't ponder morality; it doesn't
ask: was I a good squirrel?
While the sun slips under its soft blanket,
the squirrels don't bed down and pray.
They don't rise with the tender morning light
and decide to be good.

They wake and eat and live.
A miracle.

Arcadia

The men rise early to work.
Calloused fingers button shirt,
Lace up leather work boots.
Coffee is poured into
Thermoses, dirty mugs.

All day work is done with
Animals or machinery.

They return at dusk and
Groan from their trucks
And eat their dinner
And talk to their kids,
Make love to their wives.

Set the alarm for four thirty.
Crawl naked into bed.

Asleep before head hits pillow.

Splash Pad

The women stand at the splash pad watching their children. The children scream and squeal, surprised every time water gushes out from the small ground spigot.

There are husbands sometimes. They sit in the shade at the picnic tables and play with the babies, make small-talk with the other men. It's a day off work, and the day is spent up relaxing and watching the kids run around the splash pad.

The morning was lazy. No church save for the adoration of the two of them, alone, kids in the next room watching cartoons, and the benediction of "put it right here and keep going; don't stop."

The Cat the Nightmaid

My son—
He's scared to sleep at night in his bed.
It's because he doesn't trust the dark.
Daytime he's fine. He's in and out.
Come night it's a different story.
He's timid and asks to sleep in our
bed. Some nights we let him.
Other nights, the nights we say no, he
asks for the cat to come sleep
with him.

The cat doesn't stay put long before
slinking off into the dark hallway.
The nights he stays, his tail keeps time.
He looks at the sleeping boy and at me as though to
say: I worked to get him to sleep; don't wake him.

                                        For Liam

Silhouette

The man was a silhouette.
Broad shoulders, tall, fists
clenched at his sides.

He stood in the hallway
peering into my room, eyes
shifting from where I was in bed
to the door of my mother's room.

He was watching me watch him.

I was not afraid. Whether he was
man or ghost, I was not afraid.
Knowing this, he turned the way he
came.

Following, I caught the door before
it shut—bang!— and woke my mother.

When she awoke she said she felt
like a stranger had been in the house.

Insomnia

To sleep I take a small blue pill—
some nights two.
Some nights with wine, others not.
It's because I'm afraid of lying awake.
To lie awake means my mind must wander.
The garden beds that deserve tending—
The book on my desk, closed for over
a month—
Faith—
Those are nights I rise and look out the door.
In the garden, the obsidian sky is dotted with white hot light,
all jealously guarding the orb of the the
gossamer moon that raises its ivory
head above the trees.

If you're going to be a believer in God,
you'll be a believer then—
when the torrent of the moon's light crashes
through the trees—soldiers on duty—
and pools in the yard.

The Picture

There's a picture of me as a small boy tucked away someplace
in an album someplace tucked away in a closet at my
mother's house. I'm driving a toy car propelled by pedals.
We're at grandma's house. She's in the picture too.
It must be cold, but not too cold, October
maybe, because she's wearing a black
insulated vest. The trees in the background have lost most of
their leaves. Grandma's mouth is open; the camera caught her
in mid-sentence trying to get my attention for the picture.
It is, perhaps, my first test drive in the car.

I don't know the whereabouts of my father or grandfather.
I know it's my mother behind the camera. Back then,
wherever I was, she was near. The men could be inside the
house at the table drinking coffee or down at the Wabash
watching the water hug the banks, willing itself to break free.

The Cat Doesn't Like Being Shut Out.

When the door closes, he stands and stretches
in the sun pouring through the kitchen window.
Then he sits by the glass door and watches us.
He doesn't want to come to be where we are; he
wants the door open—the option to join us if
he chooses.

Morning Precipitation

Rain comes in the morning
before light and the sound
of rain hushes everything.

When the sun breaks its hold
and races across the purple
Earth, the light bleeds through
each tree branch

spilling dappled radiance through
the kitchen window onto my
raw skin (cold) while behind
me coffee brews on the stovetop.

12.31.17

By the time the ball drops—those massive New York
crowds huddled and screaming—we're in the warm light
of the kitchen clinking glasses. There's the tradition of a kiss.
Someone told me once that what you do on New Year's Eve,
you'll do the rest of the year.
This is why no one wants to argue.

1/1/18

My resolution is Tennyson.
Ring out, wild bells.
This and just only this.

1/2/18

This year we choose to be happy. Somehow, we'll do this.
It's like chasing a ghost. It's this way for some people.
I'll tell you something: life and death
happen in syncopated rhythm.
This is the year to swill silence.

Violence: Metamorphosis

We woke before sun up to fog so dense
it had swallowed the town below whole.
A delicate cold had settled in overnight
making the world look brittle. From
the french door windows we saw that
frost had spread over the roof next door.

Like hope after violence, the fog lifts
by midday and evaporates. The town emerges,
blinking, and the cars from here look
like a child's playthings.

About the Author

Kyle Doty is the author of Hush, Don't Tell Nobody and Winter Lightning. He works at a virtual school from his home office where he is managed by two imperious felines, Catticus Finch and Thatcher. Kyle is, at times, a freelance writer and editor. He is also a doctoral student at Southeastern University studying curriculum and instruction. Kyle lives in rural Florida with his family.

www.ingramcontent.com/pod-product-compliance
Lightning Source LLC
Chambersburg PA
CBHW020254090426
42735CB00010B/1925